Congratulations!

You are the newest member of the All-Time Awesome Search Patrol. As part of the Team, your mission is to find the objects hidden in each of the stories. After all, where would the children of Israel be without their manna , or Daniel without the lions, or John the Baptist without his locusts and wild honey?

We're sure you'll do a terrific job and learn a lot about God and His love in the process. And you can double your fun by inviting a friend to join the hunt!

Let the Search Begin!

The All-Time Awesome Bible Search

SANDY SILVERTHORNE

Stories retold by
Karen Mezek

HARVEST HOUSE PUBLISHERS
Eugene, Oregon 97402

ADAM & EVE

In the beginning God created the heavens and the earth. At His command trees sprang up and branches shot out loaded with fruit  and berries . Giant whales appeared in the sea and tiny insects popped out of the ground. From the largest wrinkly elephant to the smallest creepy-crawly , God filled the earth with animals.

But something was missing! God needed someone to watch over His wonders. From the dust of the ground God made Adam, and from Adam's rib God made Eve.

Adam and Eve had everything anyone could want. But were they content? No! They wanted to eat fruit from the one tree in the Garden that God had told them to leave alone.

To make matters worse, a crafty snake whispered lies to Eve. "Take the fruit!" it tempted. "You will become gods!"

Eve's mouth watered... her hand reached out. She bit into the fruit and Adam did the same. Instantly they knew they had done something very wrong. Overcome with shame, the man and woman gathered fig leaves to cover themselves.

Of course their Creator knew what had happened. God made clothes from animal skins to cover their nakedness. Then He sent Adam and Eve out of the Garden of Eden.

Sin had fallen upon the earth.

MOSES

"Save us! Save us!" The cry of God's people, enslaved in Egypt, rose to heaven. God heard their voices and sent His servant Moses to deliver them. With Aaron by his side, Moses demanded that Pharaoh let God's people go.

Pharaoh laughed. "Who is the Lord?" he sneered. To show his contempt, he ordered them to work even harder and took away the straw they needed to make bricks. Whipped and taunted by the taskmasters God's people despaired of ever being free.

Moses came before Pharaoh once more. As a sign from God, Aaron threw his staff to the ground and it became a serpent.

"Every magician knows that trick!" scoffed Pharaoh. Sure enough, his magicians performed the same feat.

Because Pharaoh refused to obey, God unleashed a terrifying series of plagues on his kingdom. The Nile River was turned to blood; the country was overrun with frogs; then lice; then flies; then a horrible pestilence. The tormented Egyptians broke out in open sores; they were bombarded with hail, invaded by locusts, and covered in darkness.

Pharaoh paced the cold halls of his palace, his pride unchanged. So God sent the most terrible punishment of all. In the dead of night the firstborn of every household was killed—including Pharaoh's own son. Only the Israelites were spared.

The Egyptians had suffered enough. "Leave, or we will *all* die!" they cried. Even the hard-hearted spirit of Pharaoh was broken, and he gave the Israelites their freedom at last.

MANNA

The children of Israel were angry with God. Lost in the hot desert, they were fainting with hunger. "Has God brought us out of Egypt to starve in the wilderness? At least Pharaoh fed us!"

God heard the cries of His people. He appeared in a cloud of glory and gave Moses and Aaron His instructions. "Tell those grumblers I will rain bread from heaven in the mornings and meat in the evenings, for I am the Lord your God!"

With the setting sun came a flock of fat, tasty quail. The hungry Israelites caught the birds and gobbled them up. The next morning, a breakfast of manna lay scattered across the desert. Greedily the people ate delicious bread. It tasted like wafers filled with honey.

"Don't take more than you need for your breakfast," Moses warned them. But did they listen? Of course not! The leftover manna began to stink. Slimy worms grew inside. How angry Moses was that no one obeyed him!

Before long the Israelites were complaining again. "We have food—so what! How about water? Did you bring us out of Egypt to die of thirst in the desert?" Once again God listened. He instructed Moses to speak to the Rock of Horeb. Clear water came gushing out and everyone drank their fill.

God did many more miracles as He led His people through the desert. During those 40 long years Moses kept a jar filled with manna as a reminder to not forget God's goodness.

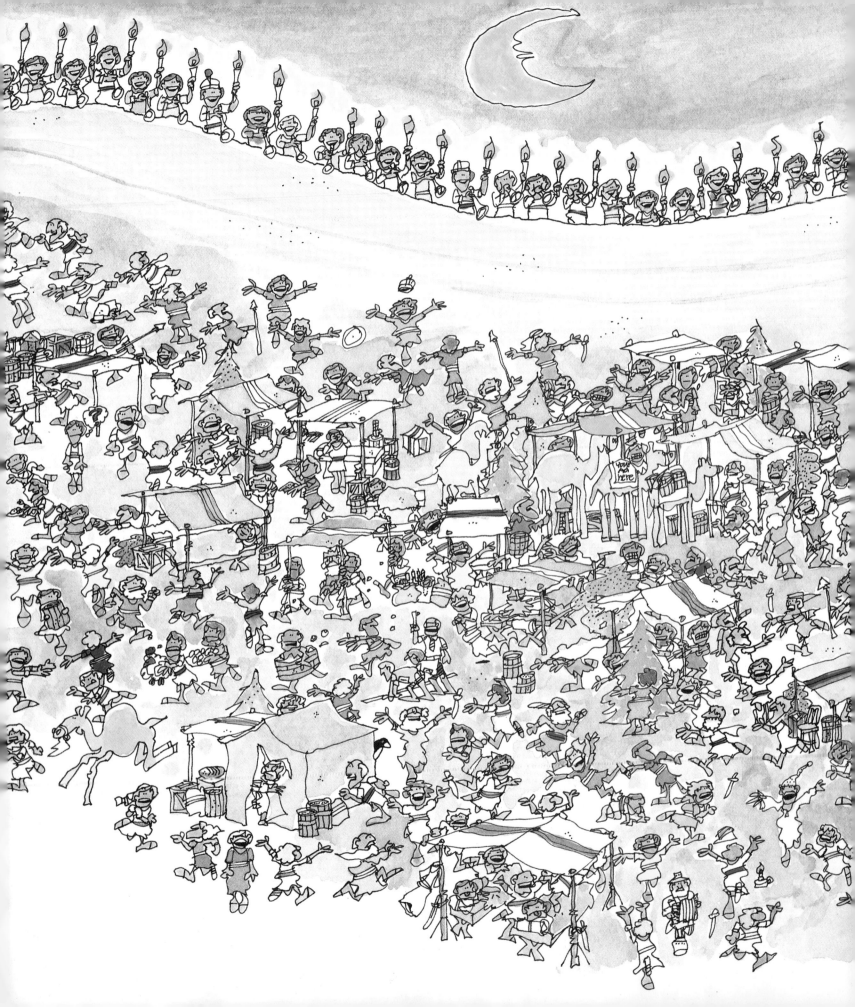

GIDEON

Gideon  looked with confidence at his vast army of 32,000. He was sure he could lead his soldiers to victory over the wicked Midianites.

But God had other plans. "Send home all the men who are afraid," God said. "I want my people to know that *I* have delivered them, and not their own strength."

How nervous Gideon must have been to see 22,000 soldiers head for home, while only 10,000 remained. Surely now the army was small enough....

But God said no, there were still too many! "Take them down to the water to drink," He instructed Gideon. "Whoever stands and laps the water out of his hand, keep. Those who bend down on their knees to drink, send home."

Again Gideon obeyed the Lord. Only 300 men stood and drank! The rest of the army was discharged.

Quiet as two mice, Gideon and his servant scouted out the Midianite camp. They overheard a man talking about his strange dream. "I dreamed that a cake of barley bread fell into a Midian tent and destroyed it." Gideon returned to his tiny army knowing God had given this dream as a sign of their victory.

That night the 300 soldiers surrounded the Midianites. Each one held a lantern under a pitcher which they broke at the sound of a trumpet. When the blazing lanterns were revealed, the Midianites were confused and ran about like frightened grasshoppers. Gideon's army defeated the enemy and gave glory to God.

KING SOLOMON

Israel had certainly done well since the days of slavery in Egypt! King David had battled the neighboring lands and subdued them all. When his son Solomon inherited the throne, Israel was finally at peace.

One of Solomon's greatest accomplishments as king was to build a temple for the Lord. After many discussions with craftsmen, artisans, goldsmiths, and carpenters, the final plans were drawn. In exchange for wheat and oil, King Hiram of Tyre gave Solomon sweet-smelling cedar trees for the interior. Delicate carvings of winged cherubims, palm trees, and blossoming flowers adorned the walls. Gold covered the building, inside and out. After seven years the temple was finally completed. With great ceremony the Ark of the Covenant was placed inside.

Power and riches, fame and fortune, King Solomon had it all! But what he desired more than anything was wisdom. On his knees he prayed, and God granted his wish. King Solomon was blessed with great understanding and people came from the four corners of the earth to hear his advice.

Even the beautiful Queen of Sheba visited Solomon's court and listened to his words of wisdom. She brought gifts of camels and spices and gold and jewels, and told him everything that was on her heart. When the queen left, she was convinced that Solomon was truly the wisest man on earth.

THE FOUR LEPERS

King Benhadad  of Syria was a bully who loved to pick fights. He and his army made war against Samaria and besieged the city. The siege caused a terrible famine and people began to starve. The people ate every scrap of food they could find—even the head of a donkey sold for many pieces of silver. When the king of Israel heard the desperate things his people were doing to stay alive, he was so angry he tore his clothes and covered himself with sackcloth and ashes.

Blaming everything on God, the king of Israel seized the prophet Elisha, determined to kill him. But God's prophet stood before the king and prophesied, "Tomorrow fine flour  *(find 6)* and barley will overflow in the gates of Samaria." The words sounded so absurd that one of the counselors laughed and made fun of the prophet. Elisha looked at the man and spoke these words, "You will see the miracle, but you won't eat any of it."

As twilight fell, four lepers crept into the camp of the Syrians. To their amazement the camp was deserted! God had sent an imaginary army of soldiers, horses, and chariots to scare the Syrians away. Hurrying from tent to tent, the lepers carted off as much gold , silver , and clothing as they could carry. Then suddenly they stopped. "It's wrong for us to keep this to ourselves!" they cried. Without wasting another moment they hurried back to Samaria to share the good news.

Elisha's prophecy was fulfilled, but the counselor who had laughed at him was trampled to death as the people rushed through the gates to reach the food.

ESTHER

Of all the women in the kingdom of Persia there was none more lovely than Mordecai's stepdaughter Esther. But Esther and Mordecai shared a dangerous secret—both of them were Jews. The Jewish people were ruled by the Persians.

When King Ahasuerus saw the fair young maiden, he made her his queen. He soon realized Esther was more than just beautiful; she was also honest and brave. When Mordecai uncovered a plot against the king, Esther warned Ahasuerus and saved his life.

Haman , a powerful servant of the king, was jealous of Mordecai and wished him dead. After discovering that Mordecai was Jewish, Haman convinced King Ahasuerus to send out a decree to every ruler in every province to kill the Jews.

Queen Esther was deeply troubled. There was only one way to save her people—to ask the king's mercy. But the young queen knew that Ahasuerus might order her death if she appeared before him unannounced. With fear in her heart, Esther presented herself before his throne. The king looked down to her and held out his golden scepter Esther's fear turned to hope. Now she knew he would not kill her.

Queen Esther's plea was granted and her people saved from a horrible death. Mordecai was draped in a royal robe and paraded through the streets with honor on the king's horse His archenemy, Haman, was hanged from the gallows

DANIEL

During the reign of Darius  in Babylon there was a Jewish prince named Daniel . He was the king's favorite prince. This caused a good deal of jealousy, and a plot was hatched against him.

All the princes and governors and counselors and captains went to see the king. "O great King!" they cried. "Write an edict that for 30 days if any man worships any god except you, he shall be thrown into the lions' den!"

The princes watched the unsuspecting king sign the edict. They wasted no time in hurrying to spy on their hated rival. Sure enough, Daniel was praying to God as he always did, on his knees and with his windows wide open. Scurrying back to the king, the tattletales told him what they had seen.

The king was angry when he saw how easily he had been trapped! But there was nothing he could do except carry out his own order. With a heavy heart he commanded that Daniel be thrown into the lions' den. A great stone was rolled over the entrance, and the king sealed it with his ring

Early the next morning King Darius ran to the den and cried out, "Servant of the living God, has your God saved you from the lions *(find 16)*?"

Daniel's strong voice rang out, "He sent His angel and shut the lions' mouths, for I haven't done anything wrong!"

With great joy the king set Daniel free. In his place King Darius threw the men who had accused Daniel. Before they even touched the ground their bones were broken and they were devoured.

JOHN THE BAPTIST

If John the Baptist  lived today he would probably be called a tramp! He gave up all of his earthly possessions and lived in the desert, wearing a camel's hair coat and eating locusts and wild honey. He fearlessly preached the gospel and spoke out against sin. "You vipers!" he cried to the Pharisees. "If you have two tunics, give one away! You tax collectors, you soldiers! Repent! For the kingdom of God is at hand!" Although his words were harsh, they were true. Thousands came to listen and ask God's forgiveness and be baptized.

John became so famous that people started to wonder if he was the Messiah. He strongly denied it. "There is One who will come after me, whose sandals I'm not worthy to untie. He will baptize you with the Holy Spirit and with fire."

One day as John preached, his prophecy was fulfilled. Jesus, the Son of God, came walking toward him through the crowd. When Jesus asked to be baptized, the prophet was overwhelmed. How could he, an unworthy sinner, baptize God's Son? But John obeyed and dipped Jesus in the water. To the wonder of the crowd, God's Holy Spirit descended on Jesus in the form of a dove, and a voice spoke from heaven, "This is my beloved Son. I am pleased with Him."

HOLE IN THE ROOF

"Jesus is here! Did you know—He's here!" Word traveled quickly in the town of Capernaum. Fishermen put aside their fishing nets (find 10) and mothers left pots cooking on the stove to see the Messiah.

Crowds of people, squashed together like sardines, filled the house where Jesus preached. Some stood on ladders or balanced on window-sills to get a better view. Four men tried to carry a paralyzed friend through the front door, hoping that Jesus would heal him. But no one budged to let them in.

"There's only one thing to do," said one of the men. "Make a hole in the roof!"

"Are you crazy?" cried the others. But they followed him, knowing it was their only chance.

As Jesus preached, a commotion started above His head. People stared as bits of grass and dried mud fell into the room. Soon the hole was big enough for the mat to be lowered with a rope right to Jesus' feet. Jesus looked down at the sick man, and at his friends above. Seeing their faith, He said, "Friend, your sins are forgiven."

The Scribes were shocked. "How dare He!" they thought. "Only God can forgive sins!" Jesus knew what they were thinking. Pointing to them, He said, "So you will know the Son of Man can forgive sins," He turned to the paralyzed man and said, "Get up, take your mat and go home!"

Immediately the man got up and started praising God.

THE POOL

In Jerusalem, near the sheep  market, was a pool named Bethesda. On the surrounding porches were hundreds of diseased and lame and blind people. Some lay quietly, others moaned softly, a few cried out in pain. All who were not blind looked hopefully at the still water of the pool. At a certain time each year God sent an angel to stir up the water. When this happened, whoever stepped into the bubbling waves first was healed.

Far from the water's edge lay a man who was so ill he could hardly move. For 38 years he had watched in agony as others reached the pool before him. Time after time he had tried to be first, only to be pushed away by those stronger than he. He had no friends to help him; no one cared.

Jesus saw the poor man and knew immediately that he had waited a long time. His sad, pale face showed that his hope was almost gone. The entire world had turned its back on his trouble, but God's own Son showed mercy and love.

Jesus stooped down and asked, "Do you want to be well?"

"Oh, Sir," came the feeble reply, "I have no one to help me."

Then Jesus said to him, "Arise, take up your mat and walk."

The sick man's sadness turned to joy as God's healing power flooded his body. Immediately he got up and walked! It wasn't long before the Scribes and Pharisees heard about the miracle. Incredibly, it made them hate Jesus more than ever! From that day on, they were determined to kill Him.

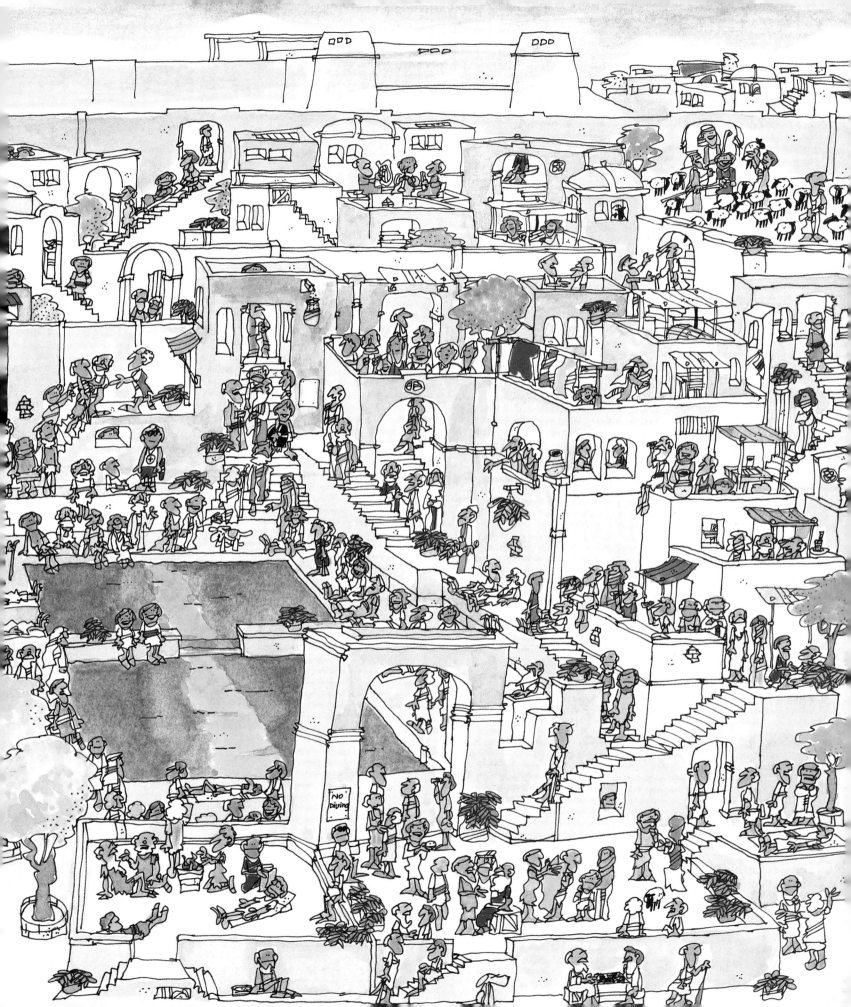

THE BANQUET

One evening Jesus  was invited to dinner at the home of one of the very important Pharisees . These religious leaders were such horrible snobs that if they even happened to *touch* a poor person with their little pinky, they would hurry to wash their hands to get rid of the disgusting dirt! Jesus decided to teach the Pharisees a lesson by telling them a story, or parable.

Jesus began, "There was a man who gave a great feast. He invited all of the important people: his friends and business associates , high government officials and glittering socialites , the most famous actors and actresses and the greatest writers .

"The night of the banquet arrived. The table was set with polished silver and crystal glasses . Wonderful smells from the kitchen filled the palace. But strangely enough, at the appointed time no guests arrived! The host sent his servant to bring the invited guests to dinner, saying, 'Tell them to hurry—everything will get cold!'

"One by one the guests made excuses to the servant. 'I'm terribly sorry,' said the first , 'but I just bought a plot of land and I have to look at it.' 'Dear me,' said another , 'I just got married, so of course I couldn't leave my lovely bride .'

"When the host heard their excuses he was very angry. He instructed his servant, 'Go into the streets and lanes and bring me the poor, the crippled, the blind, and the lame!'

"Before long the banquet hall was filled with guests who ate the meal with honest gratitude."

FISHING FOR MONEY

Wherever Jesus  went, crowds of people followed. The poor , the sick , and the needy came to hear His words of comfort and to be healed by His outstretched hand. But there were those who followed for another purpose. Many religious leaders and government workers were jealous of Jesus' popularity and tried to trap Him into making mistakes.

In the town of Capernaum some tax collectors came to Peter with a difficult question. Looking pompous and very sly they asked, "We were wondering, does your master pay the two drachmas of tax for the temple?"

The disciple hurried to Jesus, wondering what He would say.

But instead of answering right away, Jesus asked Peter, "Tell me, do the kings of this earth take taxes from their own family or from the common people?"

Peter answered, "The common people, of course."

"Then the king's family really doesn't have to pay," said Jesus. "However, since we should be careful not to offend anyone, we will pay the tax."

To Peter's surprise, Jesus told him to go down to the seashore and start to fish! "The first fish you catch will have a coin in its mouth," said Jesus. "Take the coin and give it to the temple officials. It will be just enough to pay for you and for me."

Peter presented the money to the disappointed tax collectors. Their attempt at making Jesus look bad had failed!

PENTECOST

Jesus came to earth to die for our sins. When He went back up to heaven He promised to send His Holy Spirit to live inside His disciples. On the day of Pentecost, 120 of His followers experienced what Jesus had promised.

In an upper room Peter , James and John, and the others prayed to God and waited. Suddenly there was the sound of a mighty wind and tongues of fire *(find 12)* rested on their heads. The Holy Spirit filled the disciples, and they began to speak in other languages.

Jews from many nations had gathered in Jerusalem to worship on the religious holiday. They were amazed when they heard the disciples speaking the languages of Arabians , Cretans , Egyptians , Romans , and many others. "Aren't these men Galileans?" they asked. "And yet we understand them!"

Peter stood before the crowd. This same disciple who had denied Jesus three times before the cock crowed and proved himself a coward now spoke with boldness and authority. He explained how Jesus had come to earth to die on the cross and save the world from sin. "Repent!" he cried. "Be baptized in the name of Jesus and you will be saved!"

What great rejoicing there was when 3000 people trusted God that day! Poor, frightened Peter, a lowly fisherman, had become the courageous founder of the Christian church. Truly God can use any of us if we let Him!

More "Finders" For Seekers...

Looking for even *more* fun? Try your hand at finding the surprises below.
You're so awesome we're not even going to tell you which stories they're from.

Good hunting!

 Babylonian bowler

 Answer man

 Shrimp boat

 Running the bathwater

 Photo booth

 Manna muncher

 Flagman

 Optimistic gardener

 Flying fish

 Tourists

 Cheerleader

 Eager beaver

 Bank customer

 Lifeguard

 Singing chicken

 Persian painter

 Nice catch

 Skateboarder

 Cool penguin

Temple time clock

 Ping-Pong table

Egyptian football player

 Jellyfish

 Delivery of apes

 Sporty jaguar

Milkmaid

 A hiding Midianite

Animal party-goers

 Ice-cream man

 Shopper

 A close shave

 School of fish

 An inventive servant

Trick camel rider

Starfish

 Kid in a basket

 Scuba diver

 Early advertising

 Practical joker

 The old sea captain

Ask and it will be given to you;
seek and you will find;
knock and the door will be opened to you.
For everyone who asks receives;
he who seeks finds; and to him who knocks,
the door will be opened.

—Matthew 7:7,8

"You will seek me and find me
when you seek me with all your heart,"
declares the Lord.

—Jeremiah 29:13

Copyright © 1991 by Harvest House Publishers
Eugene, Oregon 97402

Library of Congress Cataloging-in-Publication Data

Silverthorne, Sandy, 1951-
The all-time awesome Bible search / Sandy Silverthorne.
ISBN 0-89081-920-3
1. Bible stories, English.   I. Title.
BS551.2.S53   1991
220.9′505—dc20   91-12728
CIP
AC

Printed in the United States of America.